BOA
EDITIONS
LIMITED

DUSTY ANGEL

*

Poems by
Michael Blumenthal

BOA EDITIONS, LTD. ✳ ROCHESTER, NEW YORK ✳ 1999

LC #: 99–72448
ISBN: 1–880238–80–2 cloth
1–880238–81–0 paper

First Edition
99 00 01 02 7 6 5 4 3 2 1

Publications by BOA Editions, Ltd.—
a not-for-profit corporation under section 501 (c) (3)
of the United States Internal Revenue Code—
are made possible with the assistance of grants from
the Literature Program of the New York State Council on the Arts,
the Literature Program of the National Endowment for the Arts,
the Lannan Foundation, the Sonia Raiziss Giop Charitable Foundation,
the Eric Mathieu King Fund of The Academy of American Poets,
the Mary S. Mulligan Charitable Trust, The Halcyon Hill Foundation,
as well as from the County of Monroe, NY,
and many individual supporters.

Cover Design: Nancy David
Cover Painting: "The Guest" by Elena Zolotnitsky.
Courtesy of the artist.
Typesetting: Richard Foerster
Manufacturing: McNaughton & Gunn
BOA Logo: Mirko

BOA Editions, Ltd.
Steven Huff, Publisher
Richard Garth, Chair, Board of Directors
A. Poulin, Jr., President & Founder (1976–1996)
260 East Avenue
Rochester, NY 14604

for Grace Schulman
&
for Jack Estes and Shannon Gentry

Think where man's glory most begins and ends,
And say my glory was I had such friends.
                —*W. B. Yeats, "The Municipal Gallery Revisited"*

Contents

*

PROFESSOR RUBEK: Well, well, we must all have a shadow.
IRENE: I am my own shadow. Don't you understand that?
—Ibsen, *When We Dead Awaken*

BLURB

So much said about so many—
How shall we know what is more than mere chatter
among the already-intimate?
The backs of so many books are burdened
like the backs of Guatemalan women
carrying their laundry to the river
in Quezaltenango, or the old Arab
balancing his *bourekas* on his head
in front of the Damascus Gate,
yet how shall we truly know
if there is anything to truly nourish us there?

Sometimes we're lucky, and speech
falls away from speech once more
toward a blessed silence, the book opens,
and the sweet words of the one speaking
drown out the merely spoken-for
like a man who has taken a winter coat
into the desert only to find
that the air consoles him.

Oh, world of so many words,
let my book open by its own lightness,
let me be immune to the bartered praise
of others. Let this cover be lifted
as in the most perfect of loves:
just between the two of us—
naked, indefensible,
beholden to no one.

*

I. INDECENCIES

RESTAURANT

You were hungry for something once
and so you ate it, you ate it and ate it
and it was delicious, by God it was good,

good, savory, delectible, you thought you
could never get enough of it, you thought
if you didn't keep eating it it would disappear,

it would leave you as hungry as you were
when you found it, it would leave you
starved, ravenous, lonely, going each night

to a different restaurant, so you said to
yourself, *"Why not keep eating it? Why not
just stay with a good thing?"* though the flavor

grew slightly predictable, and the time
slowly came when you could no longer quite tell
if you were still going to the same restaurant,

still ordering the same thing from the menu, because
it was *really* what you wanted or because you had
merely lost your imagination, lost your appetite

for something new and specific, the sense of adventure
you once felt cruising the menu, but now you were
like a great chef grown famous for just one recipe,

so you kept eating and eating, you weren't going
to be one of those guys who went out for hamburger
and had steak in the freezer, you just kept

eating and eating, your eyelids grown heavy, your
face to the window, your old hungers circling
above you, calling your name, still loving you madly.

*

THE POET, MARRIED

Poetry cannot use a married man . . .
—Søren Kierkegaard

He missed his loneliness
the way a bird who had lost a wing
might miss its wing. Without it,
he limped about, sulked,
felt himself a diminished thing
with legs. *What was he*
so unhappy about anyway?
they asked—a good wife,
a beautiful child, a day
filled with those ordinary unhappinesses
the Mandelstams longed for . . . sex,
money, the mere uncertainties
of being. Birdlike, he slid
from his accidental nest
and flew over the city,
a temporary eagle cruising the streets
in search of carrion. But, nights,
when he hobbled home once more,
it always returned: the pain
in that phantom extremity
as he scraped his useless wing
against the sidewalks and hopped
on one leg, as if to ascend,
trying to make a song
of whatever it was he was now,
whatever it was he had left.

*

FLESH

I love fleshy women whose buttocks rise
in my hands like freshly baked bread,
arms that surge outward from my embrace,
thighs that surround me like love itself.
I love flesh that is firm and tender, flesh
that is wild, I love flesh that is yours
these afternoons when rain falls gently as flesh itself,
when all that is moral dissolves like flesh,
and only the sounds of flesh can be heard
singing, *We are still here, love, we are going on.*

*

Having My Way with You

You ride me into the late light like your good horse
and, because it reminds you of how they once
described women in Victorian romances, you say,
"I'm having my way with you." What a thing
for a woman to say to a man, I think to myself,
looking up at your white cheeks gone rosy
with the thrust of me, as if you were both Iseult
the Fair and Iseult of the White Hands at once,
and I feel the pleasure of your pleasure
and the pleasure of my own, and realize
we may all yet rise into the good light of love
from a position of helplessness, that this
may be the thing all lovers wish for: you
having your way with me having my way with you

*

AFTER

It is good to go home
and eat a peach. It is good
to put some order back
in your drawers, to arrange
your shirts, to dust
the few remaining flakes
of that spectacular other
from your clothes, and sing
to your spouse a few bars
of that old Schumann *Lied,*
"Ich grolle nicht, und wenn
mein Hertz auch bricht."
It is good to return
to the subliminal ache
of the life you are always escaping,
to put your arms once again
around the half of yourself
you have married and must now
live with. It is good to put
something sweet and delicious
into your mouth, to chew on it
slowly, to relish the taste
of it, to bless the world
in all its diversity. It is good
to smile. It is good
to be grateful. For once
in your life, you are whole.

*

THE MOUTH

What can the mouth do that nothing else can do?
Birds frolic and sing in the trees.
Snakes hiss in the grass.
If a man's mouth is not blessed,
he will never learn to sing, he will never
chant in a perfect breeze, in summer,
with someone with whom love is impossible
and, therefore, beautiful and tender.
What can the mouth do? What can it say?
Acrobatic in afternoons, it grows speechless
and terrible, and doesn't know its own home:
What shall we say of the mouth?
It travels brightly over the parks,
it dances and frets, it covers
the faces of those we might have loved
on wet, lustful afternoons, it sings
the happy-sad song of the tongue
and why shouldn't it? Kisses, too,
fly from the mouth. Mine
have flown, eagerly, to you.
What can the mouth do? you ask
Let me tell you: the mouth
can deliver a kiss, the mouth
can learn to say good-bye.

*

MIXED MARRIAGES

The young Cuban mounting the debutante from Cleveland
the mule that wants to mate with a sheep
the Hassid who falls for the Chinese girl from Akron
the canary that sings to a cage full of finches
the flute that wants to play with the oboe
and the gin that longs for a shot of vermouth
have something in common. They are all emissaries
from the world of generous singing.
They are all prophets
of a light that will admit no divisions.
They are all giving testimony
to the fact that we will come in the end
to a place of no borders,
that the way of all flesh is the arc
of a good seed's longing—
mixing it up, keeping things whole.

*

SAXOPHONE

Just as the mind gasps and dies a little at orgasm,
or this saxophone, blaring, resembles a seagull,
I imagine there would be a kind of pleasure in you,
something not to be taken literally, but savored
in small tidbits, chewed slowly, deliberated on.
Yesterday, the trees were leaved—bristling,
tentative—but today the whole earth
seems silted with snow, a future laid out
as suggestion and weather. Stormy, the night
called up incantations and ghosts, the windows
rattled like a shaken tribe, and all the orifices
of daytime and evening trembled, unsure of what
was to follow. Pleasure is something we need
to center us—holy—wherever we find it. And if
I were to find it in you, under whatever conditions,
who's to say we wouldn't be serving the pleasure
of all those around us? Betrayal is pleasure, too,
though we don't like to say it, and how might
that pleasure compare, I wonder, to a saxophone
or a seagull, some small thing gasping and dying,
trembling the darkness, finding its way to you?

*

To His Coy Mistress (II)

after Marvell

Had we but world enough and time,
this coyness, _____, would be no crime.
We'd sit and talk and eat and flirt
and never even lift your skirt.
We'd wonder how it might have been
before the world invented sin,
and then we'd pause and make a list
of all the pleasures that we missed.
But I am nearly forty-two
and know the things that time can do
to would-be lovers prone to pause
at passion's hem for caution's cause.
I know the lure when what's surmised
seems safer than what's realized,
when hands stay still and eyes undress
and safety triumphs, more or less.
But Hopkins said it, right out loud:
to have and get before it cloud,
and I don't think it too unwise
to take our caution by surprise
and kiss the thing that's meant to kiss,
and love what's taken, more than missed.

*

The Forbidden Life

> *He tickles his palate with a taste*
> *of true wildness.*
> —D. H. Lawrence

He longed for something primitive and messy,
beyond the empty blather of intellect
or the sweet balm of domesticity, something

Like a wild night of untethered love
or a fabulous impropriety uttered somewhere
among good people of impeccable manners.

He wanted it, not so much to demonstrate
his uniqueness or individuality, but as
a way back into the forbidden life, the one

He had once loved, but now lacked the courage
to live completely. His life was peaceful now;
he didn't want something that would fracture

Or rend asunder things he had suffered
so long for, and at such a price. No,
what he wanted was merely a side trip,

A segue, into the once-intoxicating terrain
he had once inhabited—a brief revisitation
of the stars, and then a return to solid ground:

the ground of human misery, and of human love.

*

"No More Kissing—AIDS Everywhere"

I hear the old man say it
to the young couple kissing on the street
and, when he does, the four of us just
stand there, laughing, on this cold wintry day
in Cambridge, nineteen hundred and eighty-eight,
as if there could be no such risk to a kiss,
as if the metaphors of danger had not been literalized.

Pausing a block later, my cheeks kissed
by the cold, my lips cracking in the January air,
I think back to what a wise man told me,
long before risk had so clinical a name,
so precise a passage. "You must remember,"
he said, "that every time you make love,
you are tampering with fate."

Now, the early wisdoms grow clear—
the serpents slither into the yard, the elegies
write themselves on desire's sheets, passion
and suffering fuse their etymological roots
into a single trunk. Why should they not embrace,
these beautiful two? They are, after all, part
of the oldest story in the world—before God,
before microbes, before the sea licked
the earth and the air with its long tongue.

They are, finally, the metaphor we have
all been waiting for: standing, in winter,
on a cold corner in this village of the intellect,
dreaming their way into the next life,
breathing air into each other's lungs,
kissing their way toward heaven till they die.

*

FALLING ASLEEP AT THE EROTIC *MOZI*

Budapest, January 1995

Because I want to watch them do what I would like to do
if I were free, and because it is late and I am tired
and out for what I say is my nightly walk, I stop
at the Erotic *Mozi* on Hegedus Gyula Street, and slide past
the thirty-minute, sixty-minute, ninety-minute videos, the promises
of bondage and rectal penetration, of threesomes and
twosomes and sums of all colors and kinds: the Black man
doing it to the white girls, the white girls to each other,
a world of cocks, cunts, sphincters, and easy riders,
and pay my 140 forints at the register, pushing my way
into the small, dark theater where men mostly older than I am
are sitting in raincoats and mufflers, in sweaters and T-
shirts, chewing and pondering, watching and fidgeting
over the dirty talk (mostly in German), the thrusts
and counterthrusts punctuated by the periodic squirtings
of seed, occasionally landing on a stray cheek,
a breast, a shoulder, a thigh, rubbed like a salve
into the skin of their targets, sometimes licked
from their fingers, until slowly I find myself,
like an old champion back at Wimbledon after twenty-five years,
dozing off, then waking again, comparing my backhand
to the younger competitors', checking the spectators
for someone I might have loved, and, since everything
becomes metaphor in the end, I enact here, too,
the metaphoric whole: I lean back into my seat.
I hunger. I fidget. I daydream. I fall asleep.

*

TOO MUCH

So much of love is love of love.
—V. S. Pritchett

So much of love is love of love:
so many birds can sing all day
so much of air is breathed in vain
love should be mute, or go away.

So much of praise is love of praise
so much of dancing goes nowhere
so much of hunger is a lack
so much is full that should be bare.

So much of rage is love of rage
so much of passion, high on high
so much of lust will disappear
when wings no longer care to fly.

So much of me is what you're not
so much of you merely a wish
so much is gone that should be there
too much is lacking in this dish.

I've had enough of love of love
I've had enough of hate of hate
I've been unhinged for much too long:
I'm banging shut love's rusty gate.

*

For I Have Lived Like a Dusty Angel

And the muddy waters have washed over me,
coating my large wings with soot, clouding my eyes,
and the raging blood has coursed through my veins,
flooding the flatlands of virtue and decency,
ravaging the structures, inundating the houses,
shattering the windows, and I have grown heavy
with my deeds, and light with desire,
been betrayer and betrayed, wounder and wounded,
taken my turn at whatever was possible
bad father good father infidel satyr
been decent, forgiving, tender, wounding,
whoremonger exile patriot rake.
I have shaken the birches, made love
under the sycamore, wept beneath the willow;
I have trembled with desire
beside the mock orange. (What good am I
to anyone, I ask, if I'm not good
to myself? Why pray to an invisible God
if I can't please the beckoning flesh?)
And what more can a man ask of his body
but that it confess to everything? Sad bird,
this human one, but happy in exile: a confusion
of tongues, a mottle of trembling needs,
the dust still gathering on these broken wings—
the darkness, the hunger, the flickering soot.

*

II. DECENCIES

ANGELS

Budapest, New Year's 1996

The years are angels: they know nothing
of the evils man perpetrates—
dead children and battered wives, justice
perpetually gone astray
like a car without a driver, a drunk
careening this way and that
on the slushy streets, who will
sooner or later wind up
like a pile of old rags
in a corner somewhere.
No, the years are a kind
of saint: they neither fret
nor worry, but simply pass
like a shepherd's flock crossing a stream
in a small Hungarian village,
like a shot of *palinka*
that soothes as it destroys,
a kindness that survives
merely to be passed around,
then past. Yes, the years
are angels, as we might have been
in another world, and must try,
and fail, to be in this one. Anywhere
that makes the relentless heart
relent, friends, can be your home.
There are things to remember
as we wane and thrive: The snow
falls. The world cries out *I am.*
Extinguished stars emparadise the night.

*

DECEMBER DAYS

Things work: the days grow cold,
buildings rise up and collapse, lust
seems a memory, then it returns.
Oh well, the day's yours—why not
make a small mess, a puddle of contrition
somewhere? Even birds stumble occasionally,
on a tricky branch, hidden from view.
And if it's ever marvelous
to have been born, why not today?

Yesterday, you were a moralist—
things seemed somber, judgmental. But
today you're heavenly, like sunrise:
everything you ever knew of good & evil
is just foam, now, in the steamed milk
that's the cloudcover over your cappuccino.
And, as for your childhood—well,
why not forget it? So you were
miserable once. *Wasn't everyone?*

Today, there's frost on the windows,
the abandoned nests of birds
are dangling in the trees, waiting
to be identified. Silly boy, it's not
only Bach who wrote a *Magnificat,*
but everyone who can compose
out of the duff and detritus of his life
a single day, a karma realized,
a rapture of one's own.

*

THE REAL

I want to go back to that time after Michiko's death
when I cried every day among the trees. To the real.
—Jack Gilbert, "Measuring the Tyger"

When your wife Michiko died,
you wept every day for two years.
You wept at the sad movies
and you wept during the comedies,
you wept while doing the dishes
and you wept even while making love,
as if love weren't weeping enough.
You wept in the shower, as the water
poured over you, and you wept
in the garden, watching
the crocuses bloom in April
only to die again in May. You wept
at the emptiness of plenitude, and wept
again at the plenitude latent
in every emptiness. You wept
at your best friends' houses, and wept
in the tedious parlors of strangers.
You wept until you were wet
with your own juices, your tears
raining down on you like petals.
If feeling were wealth, then you
were a millionaire, drenched
in its dubious dollars.
In tears of grief and of love.
Of grief over love.

*

THIS BLESSING

Last night I turned in the bed to find you
and you were there, with your body of deep light
and a second heartbeat beating inside you.
I didn't know what to do, out of hunger
and gratitude, so I merely held you,
body that was not my body, scent
that was not my scent, and listened
to the mixed angels of sleep and oblivion
as they sang in the traffic of the bewitching hours.
I went to hold you, as lovers who have woken
to their own, inexplicable sadness will,
and felt you, entirely other and entwined,
seed to my seed, breath to my breath, dreams
spiraling to meet my dreams. Who has not wept
that love can offer so little? And wept again
that it can do so much? Turning away from you
once more, I enfolded myself again in the sleep
of my own wisdom, its love and its hate,
its pain and its pleasure,
its merely human blessings: this sadness,
this sweetness.

*

DEEP ECOLOGY

My wife stays home and stares at the amaryllis.
She is watching it grow. For hours,
she sits like this, saying,
in her beautiful French accent,
If you wait patiently enough,
you can almost see the flower open.
Tired of talk, the disposable wastes
of the intellect, I stay home too,
until, finally, the flower is open,
gazing at us like a lion's mouth
from its mock-bamboo stalk.
It is bloody gorgeous, part
of the gods' own greenhouse,
right in our very kitchen. But,
in a few days, we'll be going away.
Let's lend it to our neighbors,
my wife, who has never read Hegel, says,
so its blossom won't be wasted.
I turn off the tape, where someone
with a voice harsh as a switchblade
is lecturing on nuclear grieving.
I circle my wife's waist and sing.
I am wise once more, like the earth
is wise, and the stars, and a woman
who thinks with her heart,
and a man. Who can afford to preach
who has not known this? And who
can we trust, who would trade
the deep echo of that flower's bloom
for the empty sound of two hands clapping?

*

PINEAPPLES

Quito, Ecuador

My love offers me a piece of pineapple.
It is sweet, and the juice runs all over my mouth
and down my chin. I tell her she is a wonderful cook—
What a wonderful pineapple she has made!

But love, she insists, *I do not make pineapples,*
God makes pineapples. I smile. She is so beautiful
in the morning light of Quito, Ecuador. We stroll
down Avenida de Amazonas like a pair of happy birds.

Now, I am here at my typewriter. All over my body
birds are singing. I run my tongue over my lips,
sweet with the juice of morning. Later, I will walk

Into the hills of Quito, singing the sad song "Alfonsina
del Mar." But, for now, nothing can wash this sweetness
from my lips, thanks to my love, the inventor of pineapples.

*

SCRABBLE

I pick seven letters and make the word *chance*:
twenty-two points, not bad for a start.
You're not quite as lucky, and counter with *fate*:
worth a mere twelve with your Double Word Score.
Fortune's not bad, using all but my "y,"
and now we're deep into it, as the board widens out.
Nights not of passion but deep tendresse,
as you make the word *gentle* for just seven points.
Our son's fast asleep, and I make the word *heal*,
a mere six points, plus a Triple Word Score.
And so, four years from fantasy, we move on this way,
lifting square letters from darkness to light.
Quietly, nastily, we've learned how to play,
as you wind up with *family* and I end with *above*
on this old, fated gameboard of luck and love.

*

CHAIRS

Haifa, Israel

I have sat all my life on chairs: stuffed chairs,
deck chairs, armchairs, office chairs, chairs
arranged on summer lawns, spread out full-length
to invite a savage ease, chairs in darkened rooms,
unmoved themselves by a Chopin nocturne or a Bach fugue.
I have held chairs, for a short while, in genres
of various sorts, have even made love, in better times
than now, on chairs in blissed places whose names
I can't recall. Wherever I have walked, a chair,
somehow, has been there waiting in the shade,
in the sun, in private venues where, for a time,
I took Pascal's advice and did my bit, at rest,
to grant our species peace. In soft chairs and in hard,
splayed out or gathered up, I have found in chairs
emoluments of comfort and repose. Once, when someone
I loved was gone, I sat weeping in a chair,
and its arms consoled me. And sometimes, in a chair,
a huge peace comes over me still, a kind of *pensée*
of nothingness I cannot live without. Even now,
in a Promised Land that can never, really, be mine,
I'm in a chair once more, a satyr who wants
nothing else than to be exactly where he is:
his ass at rest, his face extended upward
toward the sun, sharing this chair with you.

*

NEVER TO HAVE LOVED A CHILD

Tendresse. *I prefer this word to its Polish equivalent. When one feels a lump in one's throat because the creature at whom one looks is so frail, vulnerable, so mortal, then* tendresse.
—Czeslaw Milosz

Never to have loved a child
is not to know again that even the jar,
even the scattered, plastic tube were once
a kind of magic, that the Deity is contained
in the splayed juice of a single blackberry,
that out of the darkness of our desires
a light can come, weeping, into the world,
reaching out to us in such unfettered trust
and need that even our own greed and vanity
lie, for a moment, dormant and defeated,
that the day can begin as a blessing,
without history or rancor, and that even
the petulant sirens of police cars
are a kind of wonder, a monument to being.

Never to have loved a child may be
never to know again our love and hate
in their original garments, never again
to enter deeply into the mystery of primary being
as it stumbles and dodders and sings
all over the house, as it weeps and rails
and then, at the slightest prodding, grows happy
and forgetful. Never to have loved a child
may be never to see again our pre-
disillusionary selves, those faces
gazing upward into the light, how innocent
and beautiful and enraged they once were,
and what has become of them now.

*

41

THIS YOUNG BOY WHO FOLLOWS ME DOWN
THE WHITE HILLS OF MY LIFE

Santa Fe, New Mexico

I am still better at this than he is,
though I won't be for long,
and so he follows me
down the white hills of the Sangre de Cristos,
he who wants to be better than his father is,
as I've tried to be than mine,
though the trails and rivulets of paternity are deep,
marked in greens and blues and, finally, blacks
to signify the most difficult, the ones
we will yet need to come to, and so,
meanwhile, I teach him to shimmy and relax,
shifting his weight from leg to leg as we glide,
following my foreshadowing trail
(the same one I must teach him, later,
to depart from) and, because it is spring,
midway between the two days of our births,
the sweet angels of incipient flowers
are already feeling their way upwards
through the near-slush between us,
and he is still in awe of me, as sons
are doomed to be and must, but soon
(not very long from now, in fact)
it will become his happy fate
to overtake me, to look over his shoulder
and see me falter, as it is the destiny of those
on the downward slope, facing the moon, to falter,
and he will, no doubt, relish, at least for a moment,
the defeat of him it will be his life's mission,
if not to defeat, then, at least, to overtake,
the same one who sat here this day at a lonely table
in some faraway Wichita, contemplating the moon,
dreaming the world towards whiteness in his name.

*

AGAIN

in memoriam, Howard Nemerov (1920–1991)

And now, courtesy of miracles
we've come to take as facts,
by which the voices of the old and newly dead
can be with us again, relieved
of memory's drudge and dredge,
as if you were right here in this room,
I flick the dusty switch marked "play"
and, in your pure December voice,
you enter once more, raspy, into my inner ear,
laureate of the living and the dead,
who knew the seriousness behind all jokes,
the joke behind what's taken as too grave,
you who riddled into poems
the endless mystery of riddle-riddled worlds.
Whether the acorn was a Hassid in disguise
or the ice-sheathed branch a jeweler in the sky,
you saw the doubleness that rendered earthly things
improbable and likely both at once,
you felt the blessed rest that comes at dusk
as swallows undulate above the fields,
and saw in the reversals a mere sprinkler makes
humility and pride reverse, forgive, arise and die.
Oh, friend, how perfectly you knew
the oscillations of the sacred and profane,
and now, thanks to a world in which we're
made, undone, resentenced, and replayed,
I hear you sing it all to us again.

*

DOWN DIGNIFIED

He thought he would merely continue
doing what had always come naturally:
putting one word in front
of the other, trying to make
something better than sense. What good,
after all, were words if only a specialist,
any longer, could understand them? Remote,
separate, rendered, perhaps, unemployable
by merely insisting on his humanness,
he thought, as he always had, sequentially,
decidedly premodern: *Word. Sentence. Thought.*
It had been good enough, after all,
for so many of his betters—why not
for him? Sometimes a dark angel
stirred from within his sleep
and he would wake, jazzy
with difficulty and incoherence.
But why bother? he thought. Wasn't
there difficulty enough in mere
being, the march of sequential sounds
trying to find some small harmony to sing to,
a pearl moving through the dark—
lonely and dignified and unsure
of everything beyond its own demise?

*

I Remember Toscanini

I was too young to know the voice of Enrico Caruso,
But my father was a lover of Mario Lanza
And I still remember the white hair of Toscanini,
Well before there was a hall named Avery Fisher
Or I had heard the deep, cantorial tones of Richard Tucker
And the soft, more earthly chords of Perry Como.

I had never even heard of clear Lake Como
High in the country of our beloved Caruso,
Or bowed to "Kol Nidre" sung by Richard Tucker,
But just hummed "The Student Prince" along with Mario Lanza
In the years young Liz Taylor was with Eddie Fisher
And we stood at the Old Met watching Toscanini.

There was a legend to the mere name: Toscanini,
So far from the mundane ditties of Perry Como
As to seem like the sea nymph in Goethe's "Fischer."
Or that island-stricken, shipwrecked Crusoe,
As if he "walked with God" (as we sang along with Lanza),
Or wore a prayer shawl and yarmulke, just like Richard Tucker.

I wanted, someday, to sing stirringly like Richard Tucker,
Or conduct with the grace and power of a Toscanini,
And be a hero to my father (and to women) as was Lanza,
But never chime to Christmas bells with Perry Como.
I wanted to endure by singing, just like wild Caruso,
Not just croon "O My Papa" with charming Eddie Fisher.

Now I no longer dwell on almost-silent Eddie Fisher,
Though I still listen, yearly, to my Richard Tucker
Singing his "Kol Nidre" like a young Caruso
With a Jewish lilt and accent, led by Toscanini,
Whom I saw last night on TV, at Lake Como,
Driving a black car far more regal than a Lanza.

Yet I know they are mostly gone, even Mario Lanza,
And soon, no doubt, dear boyish Eddie Fisher,
Though I saw just the other day that Perry Como
(His new wig flattened to resemble Richard Tucker)
Would have a TV special of his own, just like Toscanini,
As if he had survived to be our new Caruso,

Proving all things equal in the end: Comos and Fishers,
The Richard Tuckers and the young Carusos, though in my heart
I still hear Lanza, and will sway, until I die, to dear old Toscanini.

*

FOR CATHERINE ANN HEANEY

to accompany a fossil fish (Knightias, Dyplomistus) from
the Harvard Museum of Comparative Zoology

Up from the Eocene I send, air rate,
A small gift homeward for my young friend Kate,
That once swam in rivers, but now lies in stone,
As if to suggest that marrow survives bone.

Born in the afterflow of mountain rains,
Only to die, and be reborn again,
Here fixed in sandstone, this strange Dyplomist,
Exposed by volcanic faults in shale-sealed cliffs.

Strange testament to those less human ages
Enshrined here now, speechless as the sages,
This small fish, fossilized as if to show
All earth knows of beauty that mere man can't know.

*

Anti-Fada

Sea of Galilee, January 1994

Atop the Mount of Beatitudes,
near the Church of Fishes and Loaves,
my son, named for the last just man,
picks up a stone. *Maman,*
he says to my wife,
a lapsed Catholic from France
who's just taken him through
the Stations of the Cross,
j'ai trouvé un beau caillou,
and indeed he has. It's a luminous day,
just weeks before the Hebrons and Áfulas
of some near-distant future. A hawk
hovers peacefully over the parched pines
and olive trees, the sun
rises like a lit yarmulke
over Tiberias and Capernaum.
My son, powerful with possibilities,
smiles. *Isn't it beautiful, Papa?* he asks,
holding the stone into the secular light.
Isn't it beautiful?

*

48

I Do Not Care Where Goodness Comes From

Whether from some subliminal ache
or a rapturous need, from the humility of Ruth
or the dull patience of Job. I do not care
if goodness comes from the deepest fatigue
or the oracles of Minsk. I do not care
if goodness gathers no heat
among the conflagrations of fame
or the raptures of Babylon. I do not care
if the wages of goodness are a pauper's fee
and not even the wind will pause
to collect its refuse. I do not care
if I must beat my head like a stone
against the doors of evil until I am black-
and-blue and deflated as a paper bag.
I do not care if I am called sentimental
all of my life (or manly or womanly
or childish or simpleminded). I do not care
if I am not asked to contribute to the anthologies
on the morality of form, and can find no home
for the morality of content. I do not care
if I am excluded from the Valhalla
of the seekers of truth. No, I do not care,
even if I have failed to look
into the image of my own poor face
and missed the center of this human world:
these satanic fires burning in my eyes.

*

FIDELITIES

. . . the one shelter, the one gift: to sleep
together. Here. Now.
—John Berger

I can see them everywhere,
smiling at me on trains and sidewalks,
and they are still beautiful. Here
is the one with the body better than yours,
and there, *there* is the one
who can quote Hölderlin in French
while doing push-ups. Here
is the one whose breasts will never sag,
and there is the one who would never draw
attention to my own emptiness, God bless
her blindness. But I have known
the sadness of comparisons, that death
is not defeated by a loud grunt
delivered to a stranger at midnight.
So I pass with the ease of a man
come happily into his second poverty,
the cold wisdom of the oft-defeated.

O love, we are surrounded by those
we'd be happier with, in another life.
But let's stay together anyway, just
for the fun of it. Let's wake
to the same face so often
we fatigue of our own singleness
and cry out: *You!* Let's sleep
until we've lisped each other's name so deep
into the low moans of habit and dreaminess
that not even the forethought of our aftermath
can tear us apart. Let's die
in the same bed nightly, over and over
until we die for real.

*

ANSWERS

Since there are no living angels, why shouldn't
I love you? So many things can sing, as flesh can,
though it grows cold and unrousable over time.

We sing, and it's funny, how easily we mount and
dismount each other, afternoons when all the rest
of the world must be thinking of doing likewise.

You laugh at my jokes, and what more can a man want
who loves laughter? After all, nothing's perfect,
not even this poem, though in more capable hands

it might like to be. But I'm no angel, just someone
who'd love to have more than one body and writes
poems as a way of weeping about it to music.

Today, in the sauna, there was a dwarf, and I,
dwarfed by my own inability to see him as human,
stopped and stared, proud for a moment at being

larger than someone. Everywhere, some small victory
awaits us, and some larger defeat, so why, I keep
asking myself, should I love you, whose calves

are too thick in a skirt, who dribbles her sadness
onto a spoon not even my lips can lick clean,
and why shouldn't I shouldn't I shouldn't I?

*

A LIFE

So you grew older just like everyone else
and the questions loomed
with their easy, alternating answers of *yes* and *no*
and then their reconsiderations,
promising us a false simplicity
like a flock of sparrows at dusk,
and you were there,
in the fragrant, oscillating light
of the good, the noble, the daemonic,
and the simply inexplicable
that might have passed, in lesser hands,
for a kind of confusion,
but you saw it for what it really was:
the clarity of conflicting clarities,
the sorting out that led to no perfect solutions,
and so you merely contented yourself
with the here-today-gone-tomorrow certainties
you hoped would lead to the right choices
(or choices you could later redefine as right):
the bright, loudly proclaimed insouciance
of the jay, or the scent of lemons,
though you knew in the end
that you would always return,
like a shoe in love with its foot,
to the same luminous starting point
of mixed feelings, the susurrus
of your one body mumbling and cussing
from its nest of desires, that old tune
of the profane and the sacred,
the noble and daemonic,
the unanswerable singing.

*

SUCH LIGHT

It was on the bus between Quito and Otavalo,
near the earth's center, that I first
looked into your face. What I saw there

Was not merely beauty, or intelligence,
or mystery, or guile, but something
better, nearly purposeless in its purity,

And, as the bus wove into the Valley
of the Volcanoes, between the smoldering cones
of Cotopaxi and Chimborazo, I felt

My heart, for the first time, drift
to a place deeper than desire, more fiery
than passion, and I knew, somehow,

I would never rise again into my old
winged ways, that all my preoccupations
with the trifling flesh were about to go down

Into the dust of a deeper longing. How many times
has a man risen from his own pleasure,
starved, for the likes of you? And so,

From the two men living, side by side,
within me, the better half rose to find you,
in a small Indian town, on a rainy June night,

And, ever since that day, everything good
within me has struggled forth to earn
such goodness, such light. Until, now,

From the Janus-faced quest I arrive once more
at that place where goodness fuels desire
like true heat, where the heart persists in going in,

Knowing love constrains and purifies at once,
Though kindness will surely be savaged in the end,
and the beast will have its way against the saint . . .

Oh love, you have such beautiful hands.

*

III. DESTINIES

So may the relation of each man be clipped.
        —Wallace Stevens, "The Comedian
            As the Letter C"

THE I-AM-ALIVE THING

My eight-month-old son is doing the I-am-alive thing.
He churns his auditioning arms
like pistons into the air,
and the small engines of his legs
begin their happy tournament
of the long climb toward heaven.

I try talking to him, but he is too full
of the delight of his own being
even to notice. He's busy
scrutinizing the small miracles
of pillowcases and sheets, discovering
the sublimities of wallpaper.

What a great happiness is his, finding
a world made only for him! And the many wonders
of flesh and fluids! Breasts
that are his for the asking! Ca-ca and pee-pee
to be made at his body's own beckoning!

But, just hours from now, my small son's face
will turn cranberry red. His legs will straighten
into the air like sticks, his small fists
will open and clench like a climber's
fallen from a cliff who is clinging to a shard.

Already, I realize, my son will be learning
something about this life. Already,
he will be practicing the other half
of the I-am-alive thing: the pain thing.

*

THE FORCES

Who, having lived more than a moment,
hasn't contended with them? You go out,
dreaming a mastery of your own life, bending the brush
as you walk, kicking the leaves. Just yesterday,
in a numinous moment, you were king
of your own book, a blank slate that could strut
and choose, a walking freedom with legs
that could say, *I am this*, and—poof!—
you were it. But, today, you're your old self
again, deep in the grooves of your past lives
like a skier come late to a mountain who,
frictionless, almost, and full of himself for no reason,
glides down the path of all who preceded him.
Sure, you've grieved and mourned, you've lain down
on numerous couches, and, still, the childhood wishes,
with their minute, occasional lisps forward,
are waiting to greet you. Who hasn't come
to the place of the three highways and, thinking
himself a free man, taken the road toward Delphi
merely to wind up with his head in the lap
of his own mother? Who hasn't swashbuckled his way
into a freedom at once so terrifying and familiar
he thinks he's arrived at some island exotica
only to stagger up over a hill and see there,
before him, the old door, the mansard roof,
the white tiles, of that strangely familiar place
he has no choice but to call: *home*. Who among us
wouldn't gladly be the chooser, if only choice
weren't a vast road looping over and over
to arrive at the same place? So why not
make peace with it? Every mother is enterable,
and every father dead on some highway to Thebes
or some truck-stop heading toward Kansas or Manhattan.
So ski down the hill, friend, enjoy the fresh air,

the illusory high, the dark fact that something
chooses us over and over until we're chosen for real.

*

LE CHAT

after Baudelaire

Now the stagnant curtains come alive
and now the pen.
Then the garbage can's the object
of his strife, and then again

He pounces on some object in the dark,
startling the stillness of the house to life,
as if the world were an amusement park,
a piece of bread he slices like a knife.

And now he pauses, launches an attack
on something I can neither see nor hear,
purrs and shakes his head, arches his back,
and makes the disappearing world appear.

What can we learn from him
who lives here, neutered,
wormed, domesticated, curled?—

How to reanimate again our lifeless world.

*

SIT BACK. RELAX. ENJOY.

I remember saying it to my first lover—
frightened, only mildly interested, a virgin,

in a small apartment at 504 South Liberty
Avenue in Endicott, New York, circa 1967,

before the invention of technique
and caution, before there was heartbreak.

Sit back. Relax. Enjoy, I said,
wanting to ease her toward pleasure

the way a man eases a lame spouse downward
so he, too, can come to rest. *Sit back.*

Relax. Enjoy, I repeated. *Sit back. Relax.*
Enjoy. Now, twenty years and thousands

of enjoyments later, on American Airlines
Flight 363 from San Francisco, a stewardess

with the sweet scent of a dental hygienist
says it to me: *Sit back. Relax. Enjoy.*

How beautiful obedience is, I say to myself,
here in midair and midlife, thinking ahead

to the other end of our long flight
when a voice as heavenly as hers is

will say it again: *Sit back. Relax. Enjoy.*
And we will.

*

LESS THAN ONE

in memoriam, Joseph Brodsky, 1940–1996

Now it will begin in earnest: the inkers
of elegies, among whom I am about to be,
the penumbral bathers in noble auras,
the accreters of influence, those
who actually knew you, and those
(always the smallest in number)
who might have known you well enough
for love, myself not among them.

You came to my apartment once,
all smoky in Russian chains, a bottle
of Bushmill's in one hand, your passion
for poetry in the other. Everything
was a life-or-death matter: the superiority
of Dostoyevsky over Tolstoy, of Roth
over Joyce, the impossibility
of being a poet without rhyme and meter.
Relentless for pecking orders, you cornered me
once at a party, asking me to name
the best young poet in America.

There were things you were ambivalent about,
but poetry was never one of them, even Auden
(the one with the nerve to rhyme *Diaghilev*
and *love*) addressed in the generic possessive.
Some said you were lost in translation,
a Russian agnostic whose every syllable
resembled *davening*. Last Sunday in Budapest,
while you were dying in exile, a young poet
from Warsaw and I were talking about you,
transmitters and receivers entangled forever.

And what of this poem?—trying to honor you
in the beloved English that honored your own dead.
It doesn't rhyme— Is it a poem nonetheless?
I'll leave it to you, to your now-cold and capable hands:
You decide, Joseph. You decide.

*

BITTER MOON

after Polanski

They are already relieved, at the very beginning,
the married couples, to know it will not end happily
for the sexy twosome licking yogurt
from each other's nipples, though at the outset
it is hard to believe there is anything but pleasure
that awaits them, it is hard to believe
they will not keep riding and licking each other
into more and more sublime positions,
hard not to believe, or want to believe
they will go on, in their black underwear
and erotic apparel of all sorts, the sex
growing kinkier and kinkier, the passion
more and more self-annihilating, so that they
are seated here now, the calmly married,
munching on popcorn, each of them wondering
what, and how many, they have by now missed
as the movie winds to its final denouement
and the moment finally arrives when, already
crippled, he takes the inevitable revolver
out of his pocket and points it, firing,
first at her, then into his own mouth, mumbling
some wise words about greed into the air,
as if to console them, the lucky ones,
that theirs is the greater likelihood
of longevity, that they will be rewarded
for all their abstinence and right conduct
in the end, and be able to walk out
again into the moralizing air, the lustless
and passionless and long-living air.

*

HOTELS

You lie in them, but are not
of them. Spread like ground cover
over their sheets, you sleep
in the ecstatic lightness of nowhere
in particular. Mornings, you rise
and grow clean with the work of others.
You will be remembered here, possibly
for weeks, for your inflated smile
and good currency of *thank-yous* and
auf Wiedersehens. Years later,
you may come again, a citizen
of another life—one that went
deeper, further, in dirtier sheets,
with toilets flushed always by the same hands.

*

The Wall

Against your tides you let a wall prevail,
A blackened thing that blocks what ought to move.
Beneath it all, the fear that you might fail.

You lie marooned where once you might have sailed,
Afraid to risk where risk would ask you strive.
Against those tides you let a wall prevail.

The things in life you once held by the tail,
You shake them loose, with all their earthly love.
Beneath it all, the fear that you might fail.

Those principles that rise from male, female,
And threaten what's below, and what's above:
Against their tides you let a wall prevail.

The moon that rose: you watched it wane and pale
Among the stars that urged you yet to prove
Beneath your fears is something that won't fail.

Those early crimes that locked you in your jail
Are past. Be brave. Be still and you will move.
Against your tides don't let that wall prevail.
No need to fear: We're made to love. And fail.

*

OEDIPUS II

The oracle said: *You will always be alone.*
But he kept falling in love, he kept
meeting lovers whenever the road forked
back into his own solitude.

The oracle said: *You will be childless,*
you will plant your seed only into the wind.
But he kept fathering children, kept squirting his seed
into the darkness of the wrong engenderings.

The oracle said: *You will be cruel,*
selfish, relentlessly disobedient.
But he kept mimicking kindness, altruism,
those small decencies he hated and resented.

The oracle said: *You must enter the darkness,*
you must learn to swim in it, live in it,
pass through it like a burrowing mole. But he
kept yearning for the light, kept flying into it
like a moth lured to its own extinguishment.

Finally, the oracle said: *You will spend your whole life*
resisting this, you will pass all your days yearning
for love, children, the bright light of your own bettering.

Now he was starting to grow tired. *Yes,* he said, *yes,*
looking up at the dimming light, his fleeing love,
his one child calling out to him from across the seas.

*

THE NIGHT FERRY

We were very tired, we were very merry—
We had gone back and forth all night on the ferry.
　　　　　　　—Edna St. Vincent Millay

We were young, we were very merry.
The stars were ablaze with desire and hope.
We went back and forth on the night ferry
speaking the language of kiss and grope.

The stars were ablaze with desire and hope.
We hopped on the ship with its turgid deck,
speaking the language of kiss and grope,
each heading toward an eventual wreck.

We hopped on the ship with its turgid deck.
Our hearts were ablaze, our flesh was aflutter,
as, each heading toward an eventual wreck,
we still hoped to love and re-love each other.

Our hearts were ablaze, our flesh was aflutter.
The wizened moon hovered, sharks circled in water.
Hoping to love, and re-love, each other,
the tumescent son and the dutiful daughter.

The wizened moon hovered, sharks circled in water.
Our blood was still hot, our id was the ruler.
The tumescent son and the dutiful daughter,
his silver-tongued words still trying to fool her.

Our blood was still hot, our id was the ruler.
In the scotch-suffused light a man could grow horny,
his silver-tongued words always trying to fool her
with sounds only time would expose as too corny.

In the scotch-suffused light the men would grow horny,
their promises lighten, their hands prone to wander.
With words only time would expose as too corny,
they dragged their young maidens to places down under.

Their promises lighter, their hands free to wander,
they slept near the breakers, they nestled in boulders.
They dragged their young maidens to places down under
and woke to fresh visages, wizened and older.

They slept near the breakers, they nestled in boulders.
They rode back and forth to the whistle of ferries.
They woke to fresh visages, wizened and older—
that had never been young, and would never be merry.

*

THE ART OF POETRY

Perhaps we are here *in order to say: house,*
bridge, fountain, gate, pitcher, fruit-tree, window—
—Rilke, *Duino Elegies*

Perhaps all we are here to say is: house;
or, perhaps, as the sun sets over the bridge
and the shade swallows the fruiting tree, a gate
opens to the thawed heart, and from it a fountain
streams forth, as if poured from a wide pitcher,
and life becomes, as we once imagined it, a window

(All that we know of the furtive self windowed
there), as if we could live in our lives as in a house,
as if what stutters out from the heart were our pictured
images of kindness and fidelity, not merely a bridge
between the light and the vintaged dark, a fountain
of mixed waters, a cry thrown from the many-gated

Chambers that swing open again, like a gator's
jaws, until what once seemed walls are windows
looking out and in, in and out, over the fountains
and the trees. Still, a man's a stranger in his own house:
he looks out at the shore, the wide sands, seeing no bridge
to the stranded self, only the old, tabled pitcher

In which now a slow, thickened, viscid pitch
stands, as the restless horses whinny at the gate
and the young girls bathe beneath the narrow bridges.
He sees again how deeply into the brisk and windowed
world he had wanted to go, straying from the old house,
pushing his palm against the scarred fountain

Until he felt, at first, like a ballet dancer—a Fonteyn
and Nureyev both at once—or like his first hero: the pitcher
who strode to the mound, all confidence, the whole house

rising to applaud him. In those days, he entered the gate
with the others, part of the large, eager, picture-windowed
normal who walked the streets, who crossed bridges

Over the sickening river and went home, nights, to bridge-
playing families and carved their initials into the fountain.
But now, a man turned in on himself, he stood at the window
and poured what he could of his life from the broken pitcher,
he looked out at the children at play on the swiveling gate
and turned, once again, toward the rear of the house

Like someone about to pitch from a tottering bridge,
over the trees and the fountains, the words for his life:
These gates. These windows. This broken home.

*

THE ACCOUNTANT

This being Cambridge, he too
(a minor in Classics from
Brandeis U.) has read Herodotus,
but now it's no longer the cycles
of history that move him,
but the more grounded questions
of whether to file *married,*
filing separately, or *married,*
filing jointly, whether to declare
one's home *temporarily converted*
to rental property, or *domiciled*
abroad, to partially depreciate
one's decline, or await the single large loss
of sale in a falling market. And then
a friend tells me studies have shown
accountants to be the happiest professionals,
forever working toward some tangible outcome
in a world already codified, and I think again
of my own scribe, Don, reading the *Oresteia*
for no particular purpose beyond pleasure,
as he follows the unambiguous oracle
of his ordinary occupation, delighted
merely to ponder the possibility
that things may yet add up to add up.

*

In a Cemetery in Keene, New Hampshire

Bolander, Blixen, Wellington, and Crumb
are friends that I've found here, so I have come
to munch on a sandwich, admire the leaves
and read Nabokov. The dead are ensheathed
here, I say to myself, resting my skull
against the marble headstone of Adelaide Hull.
Now, in the fall of my thirty-eighth year,
what I have come to is what I most fear;
a man who can sit in a graveyard alone,
caressing the dead with his still-living bone,
and find that the darkness he troped toward the light
has abandoned itself to the undertowed night
of such thoughts to be thought, books to be read
among the mute cerebrations of the dead.

*

SWITCH-HITTERS

Zlatin Bojadzev . . . surely had one of the most unusual careers in the annals of art: he spent the first half of his years painting with his right hand, and the second half—after an early stroke—with his left. With both, he was very good, though it was only after the stroke that he seemed to find his full style and power.
　　　　　　—Eva Hoffman, *Exit into History*

How many home runs
Mickey Mantle hit
from the right side of the plate
and how many from the left
I'm not quite certain,
but I *do* know that, from either side,
when the ball came firing toward the plate
and the graceful stride began
like a horse's flanks preparing to jump,
to gather, then release
its contained power (momentarily forgetting
the pain in the heavily taped knees),
there was a moment
when, in the perfect harmony
of bat, ball, body, and blessed air,
the ball would arc like a rocket
from the artist's bat
and everyone who loved baseball and beauty
would pause for a moment in sheer wonder,
the way Zlatin Bojadzev
must have paused after his stroke,
growing weak in the knees,
to contemplate the hidden blessing
that had befallen him,
before turning his body
to the other side of the plate and,
on larger canvases than ever before,
painting his peasants, dreamers,

vinegar merchants, and pigs,
while his grandmother flew off
on the missile of her elongated nose
and up over the fence, a home run.

*

ICARUS DESCENDED

I was a bird once, and I flew,
high over the clouds. The landscape
was beautiful, beckoning, a rich cornucopia
of women and flowers, and I was a happy raptor,
moral as a condor. Wherever I went
the envy of those who had fallen prey
to their own goodness washed over me,
but I must have felt, somewhere,
the tipped arrows of their envy
entering my happy flesh and lodging there.

Tame, sublimated, psychoanalyzed,
I walk out among the terrestrial animals
and smiling, moribund creatures,
with their dark pieties
of happiness and sacrifice.
*Oh, where are the bright galaxies
of yesteryear?* I ask.
*The rapidly beating hearts
of those who could never have me?*

Silly boy, who thought
he could defeat death so easily,
who thought he could live forever
in the moans of abandoned women, look
how you have joined the dark, plaintive race
of your brothers and sisters, just look
at your newly descended world: eight wheels
of cold metal where your wings once were.

*

DESTINIES

We wake, all sweetness, in the morning light
The shades are drawn, our shadows sleeping still.
But dreams were mixed and raging through the night
I felt yours too, not placid on the sill.
We touch—habitual, averting gazes,
Warm animals so filled with human shame,
Our darkness seeking out those fertile places
Which light and tenderness refuse to name.
Such subdued force beneath these tranquil waters
That lap so placidly against our sheets—
The raging sons, the too-long-tranquil daughters
Whom even sweetness, now, cannot hold sweet.
This kindness, love, is only half our fate—
Now what to do with anger, meanness, hate?

*

GIVING IT ALL UP

. . . in the spiritual world, new life
comes to those who give up.
—Lewis Hyde, *The Gift*

First I gave up the saffron light of too much plenitude,
and then I gave up the moon, with its cold glare
and many faces of armor.

Then I gave up on my dream of immortality,
with its wish for a body of infinite directions and its
sweet lusts for a diaspora of women.

I gave up on the darkness, and I gave up
on the resilient beauty of my own story.

I gave up on my dream of being Mayor of Poughkeepsie
and on my dream of being the man who conquered Borneo
in the name of the anarchists of Newark.

I gave up on my long nights of olfactory slumber
with one hand on the breast of a twelve-year-old girl and the other
on the mellifluous thigh of the wild Swede who invented singing.

Then I gave up on building the huge kite
on which a man could fly over a lake while eating an omelette.

And I gave up on my sweet dream
that the sewers would start reeking of gentians
at my very presence.

Last night I gave up on my Twenty-Year Plan
in which the divestiture of the heavens would be preceded
by a cacophony of angels in B-flat major.

And tonight I have given up on the future of brocaded silk
in which a monarchy of butterflies would conquer the suburbs.

Soon, I will have given it all up—the testimonies of light
and the vicissitudes of righteousness, the sweet angel
of no shade and the messiah of reciprocal longings.

O Lord, what will I need to give up next,
and in whose name,
on this long trek into the single body?

*

Opus Posthumous

"I never heard you speak so well of him."
"I never knew him to be dead before . . ."
—unattributed

I love the way the dead keep writing to us
from their wooden boxes and funereal urns,
I love the way poems, stories, whole volumes
about their own deaths, keep appearing, as if
to suggest that the world's graphomania continues
beyond the tombstone, that the inky heart
does not require the raging blood to fuel it,
but only an eager editor, a surviving lover
or spouse, an executor with time on his hands
and good connections; oh, how I love the way
those poems so long, "in the hopper"
at *The New Yorker* or *The Nation* suddenly hop up
onto the page and declare themselves, how
we all suddenly sit up and take notice
of those who, only hours before, we dismissed
with such competitive glee, whom we have
bad-mouthed, impugned, snubbed at a party,
but who now enter into the solemn pantechnicon
of the heroic, new subjects for our own elegies,
their solitary dates of birth having finally
achieved their peroration on pages
we now turn to with such interest and generosity,
since they are writing to us, finally, from
beyond desire and meanness, beyond dust.

*

THE WASP IN THE STUDY

It knows that window's the way out
of mind and into world, so window's
what it rises to and flies against,
as if by calling to the world through glass,
the world would come inside and be the room
and let the agitated wasp go free.

But, eager though it is, it isn't free:
the window's just a view, but not an out,
the mind remains a captive of the room
it's in, a tomb of many-colored windows
with no door to test the scintillating glass
it sets its visions of escape against.

Yet wasp and mind need something to be set against:
a chamber with a view that sets them free,
a prison built of false restraints and glass
that keeps the bold ideas from getting out,
that turns the raging breath to window-mist
and leaves its best intentions dying in the room.

But if the prison of the mind is just a room,
with only bone and glass to set itself against,
and if the whole idea of mind is just a wind
that beats against itself to struggle free,
then why not let the restless wasp get out?
And why not build a door into the glass?

Perhaps the answer's in the clarity of glass—
the way it stops the world, but lets it in the room,
although it seals the forest and the lake forever out,
and sees its own transparency as what to be against.
Perhaps the fact is neither mind nor wasp is free,
both merely captives of the raging wind,

And, as the wind beats hard against the glass,
and captive light patrols the bright, constraining room,
the mind that once was free, now wasp, conceives its noble exit out.

*

IV. DEMOCRACIES

GENDER STUDIES

A cricket chirps in the grass.
Another cricket, all ears,
joins him. Now there are two.
Up above, birds shriek
like drunken gods, the air
is atizzy with the melodrama
of what is about to be.
The two crickets
eye each other
out of the corner
of their cricket eyes.
Each desires something
the other has, each
abhors its own desire.
After a brief silence,
there will be a little
cricket mating, a little
cricket hate, a little
cricket love. Soon,
the air will be abuzz
with the sounds
of heavy cricket breathing,
legs rubbing together,
the sound of war in the air
in cricketese,
a subject for specialists.

*

The Scribes

*The earth is degenerating in these latter days. There are
signs that the world is speedily coming to an end. Bribery
and corruption abound. The children no longer obey their
parents. Every man wants to write a book, and it is evident
that the end of the world is rapidly approaching.*
            —chiseled into an Assyrian tablet,
                c. 2800 B.C.

Your neighbor has written a book.
Your neighbor's wife, too, has written a book,
and your mailman and your landlord and your maid
and the young girl who bakes pies
at the Stop & Shop—yes, she too
has written a book. Your best friend
is writing a book about the book
your first wife wrote, so you smile
and say *I'm so sorry,*
I haven't read your new book
to everyone you run into, just in case.

Once, you lived in a world of not many books
and were a happy bird: the earth
was a place of wide margins, little text.
Now, though, you're deep in the bookish dark
and ink runs through your heart like lead
with only the distant, the partial, and the dead
to call you brother. You whirl at your will,
looking for air in this hardbound,
hard-edged place of too much thinking.

Oh, friends, I love you all,
but long for a little heart
among these hard-won pages.
Don't read my own book tonight:
just walk down to the river
where the moon's thin as a parenthesis

and even the ducks have abandoned the shore
for their bookish houses . . .
their relentless, cacophonous typewriters.

*

The Jewish Scholars

Bellagio, Italy, November 1982

All day they rage: "What really is a Jew?"—
The dreams of Joseph or the blessings of the son?
The past just won't suffice to see them through.

Despised by history, suspicious of the new,
They wrack their hearts for where they have begun,
While questioning, "What really is a Jew?"

Angels of darkness, their logic's gone askew:
They think, at times, that they're the only ones
Whose past just won't suffice to see them through.

The diaspora arrives: from Poland, Seventh Avenue,
Some with their very lives and loves undone,
And ask themselves: What really is a Jew?

Dark their dreams, their darkest nightmares all come true:
So many fear the night and dread the sun
Whose past will not suffice to see them through.

Lord, whom angels fear, and devils all eschew—
Are these my kin? And which the father? Which the son?
I stop and ask: What, really, is a Jew?
And curse the past that won't suffice to see me through.

*

Early Childhood Education

Because I want to educate him early
in the ways of loss, I move my son
like a fugitive from country to country,
language to language, house to house.
Easily as wind, he flutters
over the world's landscapes,
kissing the surfaces, lifting
the splotched graffiti of his toys
from box to box like a traveling salesman.
Strange cities pass, countries
in various stages of transition, currencies
and economies packaged and sold like trips
to exotic places we can never visit. But my son
visits them all, traversing the world
to a postmodern music of cities and countries,
murmuring *Budapest Haifa Quito Cambridge Austin*
under his breath like a *National Geographic*,
time zone to time zone, vineyard to desert.
In the mere seventh year of his life,
he is already a wise man: He moves
through the world like a bodhisattva,
a Zen monk, a Hassid, a politician,
kissing the hands of widows and children,
endearing himself to everyone, waving
in a universal tongue as he leaves and arrives:
hello good-bye hello good-bye hello good-bye.

*

STONES

There are men and women who have thrown stones
and who can blame them?—
What else is a poet to do
in a world with so little use for him?

But I have always hated stones
and loved words,
and held to the deep illusion
that words could wound and heal
as no stones can, that one day
there will be a revolution of words
in which the angels will come
to sing with the vipers,
and even the dark flames of greed
will be doused by the right syllables
spoken in the right places.

But now I see
that the thieves have broken in here too
and have stolen our words
and are trying to use them against us
in the name of greed
and in the name of power
and in the name of lust.

Yet I am still a man
in love with words
who does not want to throw stones.
So I merely go on,
hurling my beautiful words
against the warehouses and windows
of darkness and domination,
hoping some less timid soul than I am
will pick them up
and turn them into stones.

*

Jewish Aerobics Along the Sea of Galiliee

She may have eaten a few too many latkes, the plump girl
teaching aerobics to a group of aging women
beside the healing waters of the caldarium,
first built by the Romans, or she may merely
want to remain ample, lovable, flesh-endowed,
as she goes about her work and her pleasure;
she may be, as they all seem to be, an aesthete
of the oral, a gorger at late-night Frigidaires,
a second-timer at all-you-can-eat buffets;
she may be, as she seems to me,
the classical Sabra, slightly tough
on the outside, but inside tender, succulent,
capable of drowning a man in her amplitude
of flesh and deep strength,
perhaps, once, even a gun-toting officer
in the Golan Heights. But now she is here,
leading this small tribe of what my father
would call *alte Weiber* as they bend
and pirouette and dip and glide, they who,
after all this, still want to be beautiful,
pouring every which way out of their
still-hopeful bathing suits, bodies
made for loving, surviving.

*

No-Goal Road

... *that secondary social man—the lover.* ...
—Willa Cather

"Where does this road lead?
Where does it go?" I ask my wife,
as we walk between the sea and the lagoon
on the palm-tree lined road near Punta Allen.
My wife, a simple girl from France,
smiles. She is happy. All day
we have accomplished nothing.
"It leads," she says, "nowhere . . .
Eet's a no-goal road." I walk on,
depressed by what she has said.
I have never been on such a road.
But the birds sing. The sun blazes
like a hot coal in the Mexican sky.
Our skins smell of salt and coconut oil.
A third heart beats in my wife's belly.
Still I am sad. I am thinking of Neruda,
of Havel, of Vargas Llosa. And how,
I ask myself, have I come so far
in this life, only to find myself
now, in my forty-first year,
in the blazing Mexican heat,
a secondary social man
walking down a no-goal road?

*

LUKACS FÜRDŐ: DECEMBER 31, 1995

Budapest

Why should I not be among them?—
the old man with the face of an angelfish
whose balls sag like overripe apricots
as he glides; the lamed *nagymamas,*
their double chins bellowing out
like frill-necked lizards; the aging professors
still revising their footnotes as they swim;
and the retired seamstress,
her left hand taking on a life of its own
as she parts the waters like an injured eel.

Why should I not be among them?—
the old Jewish writers whose pens have run dry,
and the squidish satyrs, their ink gone too,
this floating democracy of back pain and arthritis,
flesh-bedecked former sybarites
who tread and stroke, who will gather,
later, in the sauna like a Kaffeklatsch
of cardless bridge players,
where I will relish the grim satisfaction
of being the youngest among them,
a man who, not wanting to resemble
his father, resembles his grandmother.

So why should I not be here?—
anticipating my own destiny,
ontogeny recapitulating phylogeny
as we glide, on impaired limbs,
downward to darkness, scrinching
our balls back into their scrotums,
hoping to rectify these God-given bodies,
cleansing ourselves of earthly pain, trying
to heal ourselves before we are healed.

*

THE HAPPIEST MAN IN THE WORLD

> *I didn't like politics at all. . . . I was the happiest*
> *man in all the world with my psychiatry, poetry,*
> *friends and family.*
> —Radovan Karadzic

> *. . . and behold the tears of such as were oppressed,*
> *and they had no comforter; and on the side of*
> *their oppressors there was power; but they had no*
> *comforter.*
> —Ecclesiastes 4:1

Has anyone ever been so happy?
You sat for hours, immersed in poetry,
seeing it, perhaps, as a form of psychiatry,
seemingly someone uninterested in politics
as you drank with your friends,
or relaxed with your family.

The Balkans, then, seemed much more like a family:
Serbs, Muslims, and Croats all sharing one happiness
where no mere self-interest could yet divide friends
who were still brought together, even, by poetry,
a glue less viscose than the dark tar of politics
or the subjects of prattle among bored psychiatrists.

But here, too, they're in power: the bored psychiatrists,
who would make of the world one large unhappy family,
in which even the poets are drawn into politics,
impinged on by history, with its own form of happiness
that no longer seems to have much need for poetry
among angels or demons, or what once passed for friends.

On opposite borders, no longer so friendly,
brought together, at best, by a hapless psychiatry,
no longer gathered in bars reading poetry,

or communing together in that old myth of family,
which, as Tolstoy once put it, was a possible happiness.
(Before, that is, we were all ruled by politics.)

The art of human happiness, as Fisher called politics—
though States (see Thoreau) don't know foes from friends,
and hardly ever make anyone happy
as they bastardize even the myths of psychiatry
dismembering what formerly passed for a family,
and rhetoric triumphs where once there was poetry.

And what, now, to make of a world without poetry?
A world where the poets have taken to politics,
making a joke of the words "human family,"
while even the peaceful bear arms toward old friends
whom not even the balm of a bookish psychiatry
can return to the couch of their now-former happiness,

the closest of families now dismembered by politics,
as friends bearing guns outrace the psychiatrists
in a world you'd call happy, just you and your poetry.

*

TV

It was invented by the gods, along with desire,
to help soothe the cock and the mind,
a modern substitute for Pascal's chair,
wherein a man sits alone in his room
contemplating what little he knows and has known,
mesmerized by cathode and cartoon, by cast
and comedian, while a huge panoply of stars
marches across the ionized screen,
anathema, perhaps, to the high-minded
and overly mindful, but, nonetheless,
soothing, somehow, to the man
who has survived yet another day
en famille and *en plein air, en travail*
and traveling, this machine
in which the gift of gab drowns out
all revery, pure and impure,
emitting forth a kind of balm
for all the wounds a life can make of us,
speaking into the sometimes oversilent calm
we versified and vilified at once
these simple thoughts that first anesthetize
and then console, while we surf, as we had
hoped to in our youth, from wave to wave,
if not under God, yet in the end
a single nation unified at last.

*

A Supermarket in Texas

They have mated an apricot
with a plum, they have cloned
a sheep. In orbit over the vast lot
of the world, they seem stoned

with the power and glory of it: God's
handiwork domesticated at last.
Eager to graft and fuse, they've made
each clod of dirt posit a break with the past:

a new fruit, an induplicatable tree,
a fish that can speak through its gills.
It could even happen to you, or me
(if we find the right doctor, take pills,

or freeze our organs in a bank).
Moseying through the produce department,
a man not blissed out can seem a crank:
Who wouldn't love to fill his apartment

with such feasts? Once, in a Pleistocened
world, the one body, that aging carcass,
the humble pear and the plum, were hardly obscene.
But now, the world's a postmodern circus

of so many concocted delectables: a quince
buttered by its own branch, snails
that can fly, octogenarian faces that wince
without even a wrinkle, cats' tails

so well engineered they can be stewed
in scallions and a synthesized herb named Magellan.
And the busy herds are easily subdued:
they eat cake, work on their abs; not even Helen

of Troy's beauty could unchill the iced quest
for eternity in their hearts: Into every aged womb
drops a fresh seed. *Be young, leave the rest
to us*, are words they carry to the tomb

of the old gods. Meanwhile, there's so much
to choose from: hybrid peaches shaped like birds,
corn that turns sweeter from the mere touch,
harmonizing grapes, a new type of bean curd

that cures impotence and heartache, chickens
that are entirely meat-free. O life, blessed
with such plenitude even the great Charles Dickens
himself might sing *Gloria!* in these well-dressed,

richly adumbrated, aisles. So why complain?
World of invention and richesse, close-cropped
and beautiful girls more greased and modern than Spain
or any Mediterranean backwater can offer? I've dropped

my retrograde attitude of resistance: I'll eat
a plumcot for dessert, join a health club, surf
the Net, allow some playful surgeon to defeat
death with my face, keep going on sheer nerve,

as God is my witness, or these witnesses my God.

*

NOTES

"After" (page 21): "*Ich grolle nicht und wenn mein Herz auch bricht.*"—"I don't complain, although my heart is breaking." From the *Book of Songs* by Heinrich Heine and the *Dichterliebe* (*Poet's Love*) song cycle by Robert Schumann.

"Lukacs Fürdő" (page 93): The poem is set in one of the many curative mineral baths of Budapest, this one known for its traditional clientele of elderly Jewish writers and intellectuals, as well as for the metal plaques in several languages mounted on its outside wall, declaiming the water's curative powers for arthritis and lumbago.

nagymama (Hungarian, pronounced "nahg-mama")—grandmother

*

Acknowledgments

Some of the poems in this collection have previously appeared in the following magazines, periodicals, and books, whose publishers and editors I wish to thank for their confidence in my work. On occasion, poems have been further revised, or titles changed, since the time of their original publication:

AGNI: "I Remember Toscanini";

The American Scholar: "December Days";

The American Voice: "Anti-Fada";

The Antioch Review: "Opus Posthumous";

The Boston Review: "The Scribes (as "Cambridge");

The Café Review: "The Jewish Scholars," "The Mouth";

Chachalaca Poetry Review: "Less Than One";

The Colorado Quarterly: "Pineapples," "The Wall";

DoubleTake: "Again," "Angels";

The Harvard Review: "For Catherine Ann Heaney";

The Idaho Review: "Answers," "Chairs," "Destinies," "Fidelities," "For I Have Lived Like a Dusty Angel," "The Forbidden Life," "Giving It All Up," "The Happiest Man in the World," "The-I-Am-Alive-Thing," "*Le Chat*," "The Night Ferry," "No-Goal Road," "Stones," "This Blessing";

The Jewish Quarterly: "Jewish Aerobics Along the Sea of Galilee";

The Massachusetts Review: "The Wasp in the Study";

Michigan Quarterly Review: "A Supermarket in Texas," "Switch-Hitters";

The Nation: "I Do Not Care Where Goodness Comes From";

The Paris Review: "Falling Asleep at the Erotic *Mozi*";

Poetry: "The Accountant," "The Forces," "Never to Have Loved a Child";

Prairie Schooner: "Down Dignified," "Icarus Descended," "Lukacs Fürdo: December 31, 1995," "Saxophone";

The Southwest Review: "Early Childhood Education," "In a Cemetery in Keene, New Hampshire";

Verse: "The Art of Poetry."

"This Blessing" was first published in *To Woo & To Wed: Poets on Love and Marriage*, Michael Blumenthal, ed. (Poseidon Press, 1992); "No More Kissing—AIDS Everywhere" in *Poets for Life: Seventy-six Poets Respond to AIDS*, Michael Klein, ed. (Persea Books, 1992); "The Forbidden Life" appeared in Di*Verse*City, published annually by The Austin International Poetry Festival; "Deep Ecology" was originally published in *Poems for a Small Planet: Contemporary Nature Poetry*, Robert Pack and Jay Parini, eds. (University Press of New England, 1993).

"December Days" is for Helen Vendler; "The Real" for Jack Gilbert; "Deep Ecology" for John Mack; "The Night Ferry" for James Atlas; "The Accountant" for Leslie Epstein and Donald Jamieson; "Switch-Hitters" for Eva Hoffman; "This Blessing," "Pineapples," "Scrabble," and "Such Light" are for Isabelle.

Over the years, numbers of my elders, and betters—including Grace Schulman, to whom this book is affectionately dedicated—have shown me the sort of kindness and generosity, sometimes beyond my deserving, for which mere words can't compensate. I would like, at the very least, to name some of them here: Howard Nemerov, Anthony Hecht, Maxine Kumin, Leslie Epstein, W. D. Snodgrass, Monroe Engel, Seamus Heaney, Robert Kiely, John Mack, Sacvan Bercovitch, György Konrád, David Wellbery, and Helen Vendler. And to Thom Ward, Steve Huff, Sarah Freligh, and all the wonderful people at BOA Editions, my deep gratitude for having rescued me from the pantechnicon of the forgotten, as well as from certain authorly missteps it took a more detached eye than my own to avoid. And to Jody Bolz, David MacAleavey, and Karen Sagstetter, who were there with me at the beginning. My deep gratitude, and love, to my loving wife, Isabelle, who holds me steady in this rickety world, and keeps the birds coming to my window. And, as promised: to my dear son Noah, my thanks for his remarkable help with the Table of Contents. To all those I may have inadvertently omitted, my gratitude as well.

*

About the Author

Michael Blumenthal, poet, novelist, essayist, and translator, is the author of six books of poems, most recently *The Wages of Goodness*, and of the novel *Weinstock Among the Dying*, which was awarded Hadassah Magazine's Harold U. Ribelow Prize in 1994. Formerly Director of Creative Writing at Harvard, he lived and taught in Budapest from 1992–1996 as a Senior Fulbright Lecturer and editor, and in Haifa, Israel, as Visiting Professor of English from 1996-1997. His collection of essays from Central Europe, *When History Enters the House*, was published by Pleasure Boat Studios in 1998, and his anthology of poems about marriage, *To Woo & To Wed: Poets on Love and Marriage*, by Poseidon Press/Simon & Schuster in 1992. A former Guggenheim Fellow, he has also received the Academy of American Poets Peter I. B. Lavan Prize (chosen by Howard Nemerov), and been Distinguished Poet-in-Residence at the University of Louisville, Boise State University, and Wichita State University. During the 1999–2000 academic year, he will be Senior Fulbright Lecturer at the Free University of Berlin, where he will also be completing a translation (from the Hungarian) of selected poems by the Hungarian poet Péter Kántor, and of a book of essays (from the German) by the essayist László Földényi. To the extent that he and his wife and son are blessed with a permanent home, they seem to live in Austin, Texas, and in Hegymagas, Hungary, where, unlike T. S. Eliot, the author has never fully experienced "the joy of the difficult."

*

BOA EDITIONS, LTD.: AMERICAN POETS CONTINUUM SERIES

*

COLOPHON

Dusty Angel, poems by Michael Blumenthal
has been set using Adobe Garamond and Monotype Rococo Ornament
fonts and published in a first edition of 500 copies in hardcover
and 2,000 in paperback.

The Isabella Gardner Poetry Award is given biennially
to a poet in mid-career whose manuscript is of exceptional merit.
Poet, actress, and associate editor of *Poetry* magazine,
Isabella Gardner (1915–1981) published five
celebrated collections of poetry, was three times nominated
for the National Book Award, and was the first recipient
of the New York State Walt Whitman Citation of Merit for Poetry.
She championed the work of young and gifted poets,
helping many of them find publication.

*